Anonymous

Three Letters Containing Hints for the Improvement of Our Establishments in India

Addressed to a Noble Lord

Anonymous

Three Letters Containing Hints for the Improvement of Our Establishments in India
Addressed to a Noble Lord

ISBN/EAN: 9783744715690

Printed in Europe, USA, Canada, Australia, Japan

Cover: Foto ©Suzi / pixelio.de

More available books at **www.hansebooks.com**

THREE

LETTERS

CONTAINING

HINTS for the IMPROVEMENT

OF

OUR ESTABLISHMENTS

IN

INDIA.

ADDRESSED TO

A NOBLE LORD,

BY

A PROPRIETOR OF EAST INDIA STOCK.

Printed in the Year M DCC LXXXI.

LETTERS, &c.

LETTER I.

MY LORD,

THE recefs of Parliament, by giving your Lordfhip a temporary releafe from the fatiguing duties of the Houfe, has left you the leifure to examine, with more attention, the various interefts of the nation at this important crifis. Poffibly there is no one of thefe fo difficult for your Lordfhip to decide upon, no one fo little underftood by the public, as that which relates to our dominion in India; whether it be confidered on the fide of commerce, of revenue, or of politics: had it fortunately been otherwife, the interefts of the Company, and thofe of the nation, would never for a moment even have been confidered in different points of view; nor would thofe advantages

A   which

which have been obtained, by the exertions of the Company, under the countenance and fupport of government, at any time
have been made the fubject of contention between them.—It is with a view, my Lord,
to obviate, as far as lies within my narrow abilities, fuch prejudices, and to conciliate interefts
which, from their nature, fhould ever be infe-
parable, that I prefume to addrefs the following
fketches *immediately* to your Lordfhip.

Aware of the value and importance of your
Lordfhip's time, I fhall confine myfelf to the
mere outline of fuch ideas as have occurred to
me. The few arguments which I fhall venture
to adduce, are principally drawn from experience:
thofe of wider fpeculation, and of more enlarged policy, will be more effectually fupplied
by the abilities and judgment of your Lordfhip.

The chart of India will point out how the
poffeffions of the Englifh are furrounded, on
every fide, by the powerful rival ftates that have
been formed there out of the ruins of the Mogul
empire: the march of the army from Bengal to
Surat has fhewn, by the apprehenfion it excited,
the inconveniencies and dangers attending this
peculiarity of fituation: and the conqueft and
reftitution of Tanjore, with the yet undecided
claims of the Nabob of Arcot, are incontrover-
tible

tible proofs that, from the want of fyftem in our political conduct, we are daily adding to thefe difficulties.

Nor are our commerce and revenues in a ftate of better fecurity than our poffeffions; for, independently of the influence which our political fituation muft always have upon them, the former is now diverted into foreign channels from the want of a more regular courfe of remittance; and the latter cannot long refift the effects of an accumulating fpecie, locked up in the treafury of Calcutta; for the expences of the Maratta war have caufed but a temporary draft from that treafury, which will be reimburfed with intereft by the fuccefs that we have now every reafon to hope from it.

Thefe are fuggeftions that will have little weight with thofe who think the natives of the Eaft incapable of military exertion; and who confider the empire and the commerce of India as decidedly fecured to us by the expulfion of the French. But your Lordfhip's better judgment will have feen, in the late treaty concluded by the government of Bombay with the Marattas of Poonah in 1779, that the poffeffion of Pondicherry and of Mahé could not fave the army of Bombay from fubmitting to the moft humiliating engagements: and the expedition pro-

jected

jected from the French iflands, though now
rendered abortive by the fuccefs of the Bengal
troops under general Goddard, muft evince to
your Lordfhip the neceffity of the moft vigilant
policy on our fide, to watch over, and to coun-
teract the wily machinations of our enemies.

With regard to our commerce, the increafed
navigation of the Portuguefe, the Danes, and
the Dutch, with the reviving trade of Oftend,
are proofs, that the extirpation of the French
has only ferved to increafe the number of our
competitors; and that while individuals are
precluded from a direct remittance to England,
neceffity will compel them to give their money
to foreigners, who by means of a very high
exchange, of funds for which they pay no intereft, and of low wages to feamen, are enabled
to underfell the Englifh India Company in all
the markets of Europe.

It is unneceffary to urge to your Lordfhip
the evils attendant upon a reduced circulation of
fpecie; but I cannot omit to remark, that it is
not long fince they were feverely felt in Bengal,
in confequence of the vaft fums which were
exported from thence to China; and it can need
no argument to fhew, that whether the fcarcity
of money be occafioned by the fending of it
abroad, or by the locking of it up in a treafury,
the

the effects upon society for the time must be alike.

The short period of the East India Company's charter has hitherto supplied the Court of Directors with too good an excuse for the temporizing, undecided plan which has of late been pursued. It is now expiring, and the public have reason to hope that your Lordship, in giving it a new establishment, will give exertion and vigor to the machine of government.

It is from this view that I derive an additional motive to intrude this letter upon your Lordship, and that I propose (in my next) to enlarge upon some of the points that I have here but opened to your observation.

I have the honor to be,

My Lord, &c. &c.

LETTER

LETTER II.

My Lord,

IT is not yet a century since the Mogul empire attained its greatest extent, and was governed with wisdom and vigor, by the politic Aurengzebe; yet the successor of Aurengzebe doth not at this time possess a town which he can call his own. Thirty years are scarcely past, since the vast provinces of Berar, Malva, the Deccan, Viziapour, and the Carnatic, to Cape Comorin, were united under the government of the celebrated Nizam-ul Mulluck; yet the son of Nizam-ul Mulluck finds difficulty in keeping the disjointed Deccan subject to his authority; and the vast power of the Marattas, which within thirty years imposed tributes throughout Indostan, is now divided into three separate and discordant states.

Revolutions so quick, and of such importance, shew how much our political ideas upon India should be determined by the particular characters of its respective rulers. If further proofs of this should be thought necessary, they are offered to us in events still nearer to our own time. The

govern-

government of Myfore, weak and contemptible under its Raja, became powerful and formidable as foon as the enterprifing Hyder Ally affumed the reins : whilft the provinces of Bengal were no fooner deprived of the fteady rule of Aliverdy Cawn, than they were plunged into diforder, and ripened for revolt. The military abilities of Mahadarow enabled the Marattas of, Poonah, in the years 1770 and 1771, to revive the exorbitant claims of that nation, and to lay the Deccan and Myfore under contribution ; when the early death of that chieftain, with the divifions that followed relative to his fucceffion, prefcribed new limits to the ambition of that, ariftocracy, and added whole provinces to the dominions of the Soubah of the Deccan, and of Hyder Ally Cawn.

At prefent, the preponderating power is without a queftion in the Englifh ; but this tenure too, my Lord, is precarious, for we no longer hold military difcipline in monopoly ; and it, cannot derogate from the high reputation of Lord Clive, to afcribe the rapid growth of this power, in fome meafure, to the enemy's igno-rance in that art : this ignorance no longer fub-fifts ; every Mahommedan prince has now his, battalions and artillery ; and the creation of a refpectable army, within the fpace of three years,

by

by the Nabob of the Carnatic, not only unaided, but publicly difcountenanced by the government of Madras, proves within how fhort a time we might be formidably oppofed; for by the the fame means whereby the Nabob of the Carnatic fucceeded, that is, by employing the military adventurers who find their way to India, every other prince may form fimilar eftablifh-, ments, and no other will certainly have the complaifance to difband them at our defire, as that Nabob has done.

Good policy, therefore, now calls upon us to provide againft a danger, which, if left to extend itfelf, may threaten the very exiftence of our government; and happily our own immediate interefts, as well as the general tranquillity of India, point out to us the remedy.

From the fituation of our poffeffions, we have neceffarily been led into political connections with all the great powers of India; and from a variety of caufes it has happened, that our arms are now employed in the North, to protect the dominions of Oud; in the South, to fupport the Nabob of the Carnatic; and in the Weft, to give a Chief to the government of Poonah; whilft we ftand engaged, by treaty, to fend a military aid to Myfore and the Deccan, in the events of unprovoked hoftility againft thofe powers; and are

opening

opening a negociation with the Raja of Berar, to eftablifh a brigade in his dominions.

Circumftanced in this manner, it is no longer a queftion, whether we can withdraw ourfelves within the limits of our own poffeffions, and confine our attention to their fecurity and improvement; as we are evidently involved, under the fanction of public treaties, in all the intricacy of a wide and yet unformed fyftem : but we have it in our power to give fhape and confiftency to this fyftem ; and in doing fo, to fecure permanency to our empire.

In Bengal, the foundation of this great ftructure has been already laid by the treaty with the Nabob of Oud, which, by transferring to the Englifh arms the protection of that country, has converted into a fubfidiary ally the only formidable neighbour we had in the North. The treaty with the powerful Raja of Berar, whofe poffeffions lie to the fouth-weft, has the fame objects in view ; and if it fhould take place, will relieve the rich provinces of Bengal from every apprehenfion of danger, and reduce the charges of the military eftablifhment under that government, by nearly a fourth part of their prefent amount : as the Raja, like the Nabob of Oud, is to affign funds equal to the expenditure for the troops that may be ftationed in his country.

B   Thus

Thus far, my Lord, we are well advanced towards this great object in the North; nor are we lefs forward in the South, where every refource of the Carnatic lies open to our power: yet, to complete it, we are ftill at a diftance. The vaft fpace between thefe extremities forms fuch a barrier to our communication, and feparatesBombay fo entirely from the other prefidencies, that until we have converted the cold, difregarded treaties of defenfive alliance, which now unite us to Mifore and the Deccan, into a firm bond of union that fhall give us military ftations in thofe countries, we can have no abfolute fecurity for our own poffeffions, nor can we hope to maintain a controuling influence over the government of Poonah, without which the tranquillity of India can never be eftablifhed and preferved.

It may not be uninterefting to your Lordfhip to advert to the caufes which have hitherto kept back a fyftem fo advantageous to the public, and to the reafons why the prefent moment is particularly favourable for bringing it forward.

When the capture of Pondicherry, in 1761, had removed the laft and only formidable obftacle to the eftablifhment of Mahommed Ally Cawn in the Carnatic, the policy of our government faw the neceffity of forming a counterpoife to the increafed power, and riches of that ally;

ally; and the general state of India being then little known to us, this counterpoise was sought for in Tanjore.

The cession of the northern circars in 1765, by leading us into negociation with the Soubah of the Deccan, first extended our political views on the side of Coromandel, beyond the Carnatic, and gave us a territory to protect, not only independent of, but entirely separated from, that country.

It was impossible that Mahommed Ally could see with indifference this new connection, or that the principle which had engaged us to seek a counterpoise to him in the Carnatic, should not now operate on his part to make him oppose the progress of our union with his former superior (the Soubah of the Deccan), as well as that which we afterwards contracted with Hyder Ally Cawn, the friend and supporter of his late rival Chunda Saheb.

Here, therefore, a political dissention commenced between the Nabob of the Carnatic, and the East India Company; and it is in this dissention that we are to look for the cause of the little intercourse that has hitherto taken place between the English and the governments of Mysore and the Deccan. For the Nabob, jealous of the influence which these powers might have upon our

counsels;

counfels, and fearful of the decline of his confequence with us, in proportion to the dignity
and confideration of fuch allies, oppofed any
communication with them, but fuch as fhould
pafs through his agency; and the fufpicions
which thefe powers entertained of him, precluded
the negociation of any important object through
him.

Fortunate would it have been for the Nabob, and for us, if our political diffentions had
produced no greater evils; and if by mutual
conceffions, in fome inftances, we had always
kept in mind, that the reduction of the French,
the eftablifhment of the Nabob's family, and
the profperous fituation of our own affairs, had
been the happy effects of our mutual confidence,
and united efforts: we fhould then have had no
reafon to charge him with diftruft in forming a
feparate military eftablifhment, which threatened
foon to render the aid of our troops unneceffary
for his protection; nor fhould we have been lia-
ble to the recrimination of having (after affifting
him with our forces to reduce Tanjore) compelled
him to reftore that country to the Raja, under
conditions of great pecuniary advantages to the
Company.

But it is not my defign to lead to invidious
retrofpection; jealoufies are not to be healed by
it;

it; and besides, the present state of India requires
a more enlarged scale of conduct than has hitherto
been pursued. System and vigorous exertion are
become absolutely necessary in the administration
of our affairs there; and neither the one or the
other can be hoped for, until, forgetting past
injuries and suspicions, we cordially return to
our former confidence; and until we adopt some
honorable and consistent plan for uniting the
power of the Carnatic, and bringing it effectually under our direction.

This subject is probably now under your Lordship's consideration: I will therefore only observe
upon it, that the late revolutions at Tanjore, by
making the Nabob feel our power, and by leaving him still to hope from our friendship, have
now totally removed the cause which kept us
so long at a distance from the Soubah and from
Hyder Ally: that the subsidy drawn from the
Tanjore country, of near £ 200,000 a year, has
greatly increased our resources: and that no longer alarmed by the ambition of the Nabob, who,
in disbanding his army must have appeased our
jealousy, we are more than ever prepared to
form an union with those powers, upon the
broad basis of mutual interest and security.

The hour, therefore, seems now arrived, when
your Lordship may, and I must add, when the
interest

intereft of the nation makes it neceffary, that you fhould adopt a general and a decided plan of conduct, in refpect to our poffeffions and government in India. We are at this moment free almoft from the intrigues of the French; our army is augmented; the Soubah of the Deccan continues to folicit the aid of our friend-fhip; the fituation of the Maratta affairs calls for vigorous exertion; and the government of Myfore, though ftill animated by the fpirit of Hyder Ally, is not yet become powerful enough to difpute our fuperiority, or to difregard the terms of our alliance.

Under circumftances fo favourable, can we hefitate to render ourfelves the umpires of India? we want no further extenfion of territory: we feek no new revolutions: we are at the zenith of our power: our intereft, our future fafety, and the common good of India, all unite in calling upon us to employ this happy crifis of our influence, for perfecting, with moderation and juftice, a fyftem that fhall fet bounds to the future ambition of our neighbours, pre-fcribe limits to our own, and effectually fecure to them, and to ourfelves, the undifturbed pof-feffion of our prefent refpective dominions.

I have faid, that the Soubah of the Deccan continues to folicit the aid of our friendfhip:

we

we impatiently defire; on our part, that he would convert our reverfionary right to the province of Guntoor into prefent occupancy; for the moft profitable articles of our trade are drawn from that province, which abounds with manufactures; its revenue is confiderable; and it feparates our northern poffeffions from the Carnatic.

The government of Madras opened a negociation laft year upon this fubject with Bazalet-Jung, he being, under his brother the Soubah, tenant for life of Guntoor; but either the mode they adopted, or the matter with which they accompanied their negociation, proved fo offenfive to the Soubah, and has been thought fo exceptionable by the fuperintending council of Bengal, that it has been judged neceffary to interpofe the controuling power of that government : and the negociation with the Soubah is now in their hands.

Under the direction of Mr. Haftings it cannot fail of fuccefs, though it muft be believed, that he will think no fuccefs complete, until, with the full poffeffion of the province of Guntoor, he can obtain for the Company an abfolute releafe from the tribute of £86,000 a year, which they are bound by treaty to pay to the Soubah,

for

for that and the other provinces now in their poffeffion, and known by the name of the Northern Circars.

But conceffions of fuch importance are not to be obtained, my Lord, without fome return; and the only one of any value which we can make to the Soubah, will be to lend him the affiftance of our troops to be employed for the fupport of his government, and the protection of his dominions; that is to fay, for retaining in due fubjection thofe of his dependants, who, prefuming upon the general convulfions of India, arm upon every occafion to oppofe his authority; or thofe, who feeing an exemption from tribute in the public difturbances, cabal with the neighbouring powers to excite them, and in the moment of neceffity ftipulate with their fuperior, before they will fend him that aid to which he is entitled by the general conftitution of Indoftan.

The impoverifhed ftate of the Soubah's treafury can be no objection at this time to our giving him the affiftance of our troops, as the charges incident to fuch a fervice might be defrayed from the funds we fhould hold in our own hands; as the tribute of £86,000, and the revenue of Guntoor, which may be eftimated at

£100,000

£100,000 a year, would be more than adequate to the expence, and fhould in reafon be applied to it, until the fervices we might render to the Soubah, fhould enable him to make us other affignments.

Powerful, and confident as Hyder Ally may be in his own refources, the jealous fears of an Indian court would not fuffer him to fee, without uneafinefs, fo marked an affurance of our attachment to the intereft of the Soubah, whofe claim of fuperiority over the country of Myfore is ftill unimpaired, even by any pretended conceffion of the Mogul. It may too be prefumed that, drawing near the verge of life, the favorite object of Hyder's mind muft now be to eftablifh the fucceffion in his family : and this might be endangered, if he were to die at enmity with us, for he is ftill confidered by the Myforeans as an ungenerous ufurper ; and their attachment to the Raja, whofe place he has affumed, would probably difcover itfelf under the countenance of an Englifh army, co-operating on the North with the Soubah, on the South with the Nabob of the Carnatic, and in the Weft, upholding the government of Poonah.

Hyder Ally is too wife and too experienced a politician not to fee all the extent of fuch a dan-

ger;

ger; and feeing it, not to provide againft it in time, by foliciting that the government of Myfore may not be the only one excluded from our protection. Hyder Ally will therefore requeft a military aid from us, and propofe affignments for its fupport : fo that our very rivals, upon the principle of their own intereft and fecurity, will become inftruments to put us in poffeffion of what we are called upon, from fo many motives, to make the firft object of our policy.

The balance of India will thus neceffarily be placed in our hands. With a decreafe of expence we fhall have a great increafe of force : and our attention, drawn from our affairs at home by one object, only, will leave us the leifure to inveftigate our internal fyftem, and to correct its defects. Our population and induftry will increafe; plenty and happinefs will diffufe themfelves amongft our own immediate fubjects; and every inhabitant of that extenfive region will have caufe to blefs and pray for the prefervation of that juftice, policy, and moderation, which fecure, upon the bafis of Britifh power and wifdom, the peace and happinefs of India.

Inducements fuch as thefe become their own advocates. They need no ornaments of diction to give them weight. Founded upon facts, they are

urged

urged with confidence; and having reference to the great interefts of the nation, they are addreffed to your Lordfhip.

I have the honor to be,

My LORD, &c. &c.

LETTER

c

LETTER III.

My Lord,

IN the preceding letter I have endeavoured to trace the outline of a political plan for the conduct of our interests in India, and to point out the advantages that may be derived from such a syftem. I must not, however, conceal from your Lordfhip, that the national wifdom hath not yet relieved the India Company from one great embarraffment in their military arrangements; and that without this aid, we may, in the very exertion of our policy, fow the feeds of our ruin.

I allude to the manner of recruiting the army in India, and the confequent difficulties, not only of completing the regiments, but of procuring any men fit for foldiers to engage in the fervice of the Company; although it is a fact beyond contradiction, that the appointments of the foldier are no where fo high, nor more regularly paid; and I may venture to add, that the nation is no where more interefted in having a well-formed European army, whether we confider its comparative numbers with the native troops in the fervice of the Company, the extent

of

of empire to be protected, or the vast importance of its revenue, and of its commerce.

I will not intrude on your Lordship's leisure by a detail of the embarraffments and evils attending the prefent method of enlifting for India, as I am confident no man, who can be confulted upon it, will undertake its defence; nor will I examine why the bills, that have at different times been propofed to parliament for removing thefe embarraffments, have failed of fuccefs. The neceffity of adopting fome plan, by which the army in India may be well and completely recruited, has never before, perhaps, been felt in its full force. It is now only, that every motive of national honor, intereft, and fafety unite in calling the attention of the public to this object: it would therefore be unjuft to conclude from any former difappointments, that any man, or body of men, will now be found fo wanting in duty to their country, as to oppofe a meafure calculated folely for the improvement of an eftablifhment, upon which our very exiftence in the Eaft is known to depend.

I underftand the ufage in his Majefty's fervice in time of war is, to attach two additional companies to each regiment, the officers of which are conftantly employed in England to enlift men, who, as they are engaged, are fent to Chatham,

Chatham, where they are difciplined, and held in readinefs to be drafted, as the exigencies of the fervice, or the particular wants of the different regiments, may render it neceffary. In India, my Lord, we are always to be confidered in a ftate of warfare, at leaft good policy requires that we fhould be at all times prepared for active fervice; an inftitution, therefore, upon the fame principle would be highly ufeful for recruiting the army in that country. Permit me then to afk, my Lord, why may not the Company be allowed to appoint officers from the different pre-fidencies, to recruit publicly in this country and in Ireland? and why may they not be permitted to fix a general rendezvous, like that at Chat-ham, where their recruits may be formed to dif-cipline, and kept to the healthful exercifes of a foldier, until the moment of embarkation?

By fome fuch means, I will venture to fay, that the army in India might be made to receive a difciplined foldier in every recruit who might be fent thither; whereas, by the mode at prefent obferved, they arrive raw and untaught, and one half at leaft are, from difeafe and decay, unfit for fervice. I will affert with equal confidence, that every recruit would then become a ready vo-lunteer; for what foldier, who knows that he can purchafe provifions in India at half the price he he pays for them in England; that tobacco, linen, and arrack are in a still cheaper proportion; that the pay of a foot soldier is *d.* a-day more than in a marching regiment at home; that he enlists but for a limited time; and that, if invalided by service, he can return to his own country with a daily allowance of one shilling, to spend where he may chuse his retreat: What soldier, I repeat it, could resist such arguments? And permit me to ask, my Lord, what arguments can be urged that should prevent government from investing the East India Company with the liberty of recruiting the army for the protection of our valuable dominion in the East, upon a plan found useful in the service of the crown.

If there are any objections to this plan, which I confess do not occur to me, but which possibly may to others; yet I trust they will be found inconsiderable, when compared with the solid advantages which I have endeavoured to suggest to your Lordship.

I know it may be objected, that a mode so effectual for recruiting an army at such a distance, must unavoidably be a great drain upon that part of our population which is fit for military service; but as some effective mode must be adopted, and as every such mode must be followed by a similar consequence, this cannot be maintained as a particular exception to that which

is

is here propofed. As a general objection, it muft ever be confidered as of ferious import; and therefore I will hope to meet your Lord-fhip's indulgence, as well as the wifhes of every reflecting man, in propofing a meafure which can-not fail to leffen this drain; and which, while it promifes to fupply our army with fome ufeful fubjects, will at the fame time deprive the differ-ent powers of India of one of the principal fources from whence they now draw their ftouteft and beft difciplined troops: I mean the off-fpring of our foldiery.

All the governments of Europe, even thofe where the abfolute power of the fovereign fub-jects every man to military fervice, have feen the utility of forming eftablifhments for the children of foldiers; and they are now adopted almoft every where upon the continent, as certain and great refources. In this country, and in our fifter king-dom, inftitutions of this kind have been formed upon the larger ground of providing fo many ufeful members to fociety; the principles of our government, and the happy fecurity we live un-der, rendering it equally unconftitutional and unneceffary to confign any individual to a mili-tary profeffion before he is qualified to make a choice for himfelf.

Were our poffeffions in India conftituted as thefe iflands are, or were they capable of receiv-ing

ing such a conftitution, it would be criminal to propose any lefs liberal plan: but whilft every profeffion is confidered by the natives as an inheritance not only of the family, but of the caft; whilft the religious prejudices of a whole people are found to oppose the communication of thefe privileges to any out of their own tribes; it would be impracticable to form eftablifhments in India upon the principle of our national inftitutions.

Whether then, my Lord, by fome fmall abridgment of that national liberty which we, with fo much reafon, pride ourfelves on in this country, fhall we incorporate thefe children into a fociety, which commands refpect in every part of the world? or fhall we, by an inattention to the common duties of humanity, as well as policy, continue to augment the number of the already too numerous tribes of Pariars and Hallencores? —of fellow-creatures, born out-cafts of fociety, and whofe lives, in many parts of India, are at the abfolute mercy of every individual, whom accident has exempted from fimilar profcription!

Your Lordfhip cannot hefitate upon the option to be made. Your decifion muft be in favor of a public eftablifhment, and you will

D   yield

yield to the neceffity which which directs that fuch eftablifhments fhould be merely nurferies for the army, in which, from the habits of early exercife, the boys may be formed to difcipline, and fitted for the fervice.

The marine force of India does not lefs claim the attention of your Lordfhip: nor are the improvements which may be made in its eftablifhment, lefs confequential than thofe which may be fuggefted on the part of the military.

It is a fact of general notoriety, that the climate of India is fo particularly unfavorable to the fhips built of the materials of Europe, that thofe which are fent thither are found barely equal to the ftation of three years, which is ufually fixed for the fquadron in thofe feas : while every man who has refided in India can inform your Lordfhip, that the fhips built in that country, are of an extraordinary duration, infomuch that it is not uncommon to hear of a fhip that has been in conftant fervice, thirty-five and forty years *, except, during the fhort intervals of repairing.

---

* Voyage en Arabie, &c. &c. par Niebuhr, 1780.
" Le bois dont les Indiens fe fervent pour leurs vaiffeaux
" (Tàk) eft fi dur, que les vers n'ôfent pas s'y frotter ;
" et de là vient que l'on trouve fouvent, chez eux, des
" vaiffeaux qui ont 80 jufqu'à 90 ans."

This

This circumftance amounts in itfelf to a de-
monftration, that it would be for the public fervice, that the fhips deftined for the Indian ftation
fhould be built in India, provided the timber of
that country fhould be found of dimenfions proper for fhips of the line; and if there are, or
can be made, docks of fufficient extent and capacity for fuch a purpofe.

With refpect to timber, it is known that
the Teak wood of India yields only to mahogany in its dimenfions; and I queftion whether
even the mahogany can rival it in its ftately
growth. This wood is produced in great
abundance upon the coafts of Orixa and
Malabar; and in ftill greater abundance in the
country of Pegu, upon the eaftern fide of the
bay of Bengal: fo that whether we look to Bombay, as the great magazine for creating our Indian
navy; or whether we carry our attention in part
to the iflands of Nicobar and Andaman in the
bay of Bengal; in either, or in both events,
timber fit for the conftruction of large fhips is
to be found with fo little inconveniency, that it
would feem no difficulty could be fuggefted upon
that head.

If it fhould be objected, that the Teak wood
is not applicable to all the purpofes of the fhip-
wright; yet that will be no difcouragement, as

there

there grows, in moſt parts of India, another ſpe-
cies of timber, the moſt eligible perhaps in the
world, to ſupply what are termed the Knees in
Ship-building, in general ſo difficult to be obtained of ſufficient dimenſions; the excellence
of this timber reſults not only from its tortuous
growth, but from the peculiar property it poſ-
ſeſſes, of acquiring ſtrength and durability in the
ſea water.

How far the docks, already eſtabliſhed at
Bombay, may be proper for the conſtruction of
ſhips of the line, or how far it may be practi-
cable to render them convenient for ſuch a ſer-
vice, I will not preſume to determine. But
there are men of local knowledge, and of pro-
feſſional ability, now in England, whoſe information may decide your Lordſhip's judgment
upon theſe ſubjects. It were to be wiſhed your
Lordſhip could be referred to ſources of equal in-
telligence with reſpect to the iſlands of Nicobar
and Andaman; for their ſituation in the bay of
Bengal, between the 8th and 12th degrees of northern latitude, is particularly convenient for the
command of that ſea, and conſequently for the
protection of our poſſeſſions in Bengal, and on
the coaſt of Coromandel.

But though I cannot pretend to direct your
Lordſhip's enquiries upon this ſubject, I can yet,
with

with great confidence, venture to encourage
them, by requesting you will be pleased to turn
for a moment to any chart of the Bay of Bengal:
your Lordship will there find, that two of the
Nicobar islands are placed in so happy a position,
opposite to each other, and formed so particularly for the purpose of giving shelter to shipping,
and of offering them a free passage at all times,
either to the East or to the West, that our most
sanguine imaginations could not picture to us a
harbour with greater advantages for our fleets,
than this one possesses. It has depth of water
for our largest ships, and capacity for a greater
fleet than we have ever yet maintained in the
eastern sea. It lies in the latitude of 8—9 north.
Its distance from Madras and from Bengal is inconsiderable, and the passage is often effected in
five or six days ; at the worst season of the year,
in fifteen.

- With a port like this to the eastward, our
fleet would at all times be able to guard the en-
trance of the bay ; for in the violence of the
monsoon on the coast of Coromandel, all is tran-
quil on the coast of Tenasserim, and in the neighbourhood of these islands. The port of Merguey, to which the French retired in the monsoons
during the last war, would no longer afford them
a retreat ; for without a superiority at sea, they
would

would never venture to approach so near the place of our naval strength, Merguey lying still to the eastward of the Nicobars, on the coast of Tenasserim.

In addition to these advantages of situation, the vicinity of these islands to the kingdom of Pegu gives them a particular recommendation; not only on account of the Teak timber, with which that country abounds, but for the many valuable articles of commerce that may be drawn from it. We want but the countenance of such a support as our fleet, to revive our trade with Pegu, and to make the silver mines of that country contribute to incite the industry of our Indian manufacturers; the painted callicoes of Bengal and the coast of Coromandel having been, till of late years, in great request in Pegu, where a large vent would again be opened, the moment the farmers of the customs there should be made to respect the English flag, and to allow us the privilege of a free commerce, to which we were intitled by former treaties, though it has been denied us of late by the exacting avarice of these men.

The climate of India, though not so destructive of our seamen, as of our ships, does nevertheless, by exposing them to the ardent influence

of

of the fun, fubject them to very violent and dan-
gerous diforders. I fay, my Lord, by expofing
them to the ardent influence of the fun ; for, ab-
ftracted from that, I am convinced the climate
of India is not unfriendly to our people. It is
therefore particularly upon that account that I
am induced to fuggeft to your Lordfhip, the idea
of allotting to each fhip of war, while in India,
a certain number of Lafcars, or Indian failors,
who fhould be charged with the boat fervice, and,
fuch other duties as may relieve the Englifh failor
from the violence of this heat, and which may
be performed by the native Indians without danger ; for, accuftomed from their infancy to the
hot fun of the Eaft, there would be neither hard-
fhip nor inhumanity in impofing fuch duties upon
them.

If I may be allowed to extend this idea, I
would carry it to a temporary exchange, in India,
of the marines belonging to the fquadron, for an
equal number of difciplined Lafcars, to be re-
turned when the fleet fhould be called back to
Europe, or relieved by other fhips. We have
fuch unqueftionable proof in our Seapoys, of
what the natives of India are to be brought to,
by difcipline and regulations, that it cannot now
be doubted, but that, under proper management,
they may be made equal to any fervice. The
regimented Seapoys being compofed of men

drawn indifcriminately from the different cafts of
the country, it would be impoffible to prevail
on them to fubmit to the duties of marine fervice; but a corps under the denomination of
Lafcar Seapoys, might be formed for that purpofe, and they would, without a murmur, take
the place of the marines who might be landed,
and who, by becoming a temporary reinforce-
ment to the eftablifhment, would enable us to
make exertions of our own ftrength, at times
when we fhould not venture to hazard them
without fuch affiftance. This further advantage
would attend fuch a plan, that in the event of
any foreign expedition againft Manilla, or to the
continent of America, a body of men would be
ready formed for embarkation, upon whofe
willing fervices we might fafely rely.

I will detain your Lordfhip no longer: I
will reft affured of finding my apology in the
apparent confequence and utility of my fubject:
in its moft homely drefs, it may awaken the attention, and claim the indulgence of your
Lordfhip. I have endeavoured to confine myfelf to fuch facts and propofitions, as, from the
experience of the evils they are intended to remedy, become in a great meafure their own advocates: nor have I intruded upon your Lordfhip

fhip a fingle idea, that I did not think, from the pureft conviction of my heart, was equally directed to the interefts of the Company and of the nation.

Should thefe, or any meafures fimilar to thefe fuggefted, have the good fortune to meet the approbation of government, the Eaft India Company may foon hope to find themfelves invefted with powers adequate to carry them into execution; and the liberal exertions of the nation may happily co-operate in producing the extenfion of a fyftem replete with reciprocal and permanent advantages. Upon fuch principles the Company may hope, both in the Cabinet and in the Senate, to find an advocate in the influence and abilities of your Lordfhip; and with fuch wifhes, your Lordfhip will permit an humble individual to fubfcribe himfelf, with the higheft refpect,

Your Lordfhip's moft obedient

and moft humble fervant.

E

It]

It was my original intention to have troubled
your Lordſhip with ſome further ſketches
upon the ſubjects of the circulation and commerce of India; but as thoſe points would
carry me to a great length, and as the latter
of them has been treated in a late addreſs to
the Court of Directors, I have ſuppreſſed
them here, to give place to the following
original letter, the date of which may
afford authority, and in ſome degree tend
to illuſtrate the general ideas before ſug-
geſted to your Lordſhip.

To ———, Eſq.

May 27th 1774.

IN my laſt I promiſed to conſider with you,
how far policy makes it neceſſary that the Company ſhould interfere in the general ſyſtem of
India, and what benefits they may expect to draw
from ſuch a conduct. The Act of Parliament
you have ſent me, is come in time to encourage
me to go on : for the preamble declares, that the
preſent powers in the Company's repreſentatives
are inſufficient, and therefore inſtitutes a new and
ſuperior authority, which in all political matters
is to direct the whole machine.

Whatever

Whatever fufpicions may be entertained of the views of government in this act, the experience of fome years has fully fhewn, that the plea upon which it is founded is juft, and that a divided authority was very unequal to preferve the pof-feffions in Bengal, Bombay, and this coaft, from the infults or invafions of the very powerful neighbours we have on every fide : even this authority united will be infufficient for fuch a pur-pofe, unlefs the influence of it, and of our military reputation, fhould be improved by policy; and unlefs we take advantage of the peace in Europe, of the diftracted ftate of the Maratta affairs, of the embarraffments of the Soubah, and the good difpofitions of Soujah Dowlah and Hyder Ally, to extend and eftablifh it in fuch a manner as may give us the direction of the whole machine.

Do not call me chimerical for fuggefting fuch an idea. Could I fee by what other means the intereft and honor of the nation could be fecured, this idea fhould not long have obtained with me; but when it is acknowledged by every one who has confidered the ftate of India, and our fitua-tion on this and the Malabar coaft, that our pre-fent military eftablifhments are unequal to the protection of our own poffeffions, and thofe of our allies which we have engaged to protect; and

when

when it is as well known that our refources are unequal to the fupport even of thefe eftablifh-ments, it muft I think be confeffed, that our authority is but poorly fupported ; and that, un-lefs we either go from our engagements and con-tract our poffeffions on both coafts, or form fuch further connexions with our neighbours, as may not only relieve us from our apprehenfions of them, but give us the addition of their ftrength both in men and money, we fhall be conftantly expofed to alarms and invafions, and of courfe the advantage of the India poffeffions to the na-tion be made very precarious.

Call to mind what apprehenfions were raifed in Europe, and in every part of India, when the news was received that a large armament was at Mauritius. How many good reafons were then brought by thofe who thought a Maratta alliance moft favorable to the French for their landing troops near Bombay, and attacking us on that fide : and what confequences were drawn from a fuppofition of their fuccefs on that quarter. On the other hand, how many inducements were they fuppofed to have for joining themfelves with Hyder; and what confequences were drawn from the fuppofition of their union. Even an alliance with the Soubah, or with the Cuttack Marattas, was well fupported.

In

In fhort, to judge from the variety of opinions
and apprehenfions which prevailed at that time,
one would be inclined to fuppofe every power
in India the inveterate enemy of the Englifh, and
proportionably attached to the intereft of the
French. I do not mean to adopt this opinion;
but yet there generally is enough of good fenfe
in the public opinion to juftify my introducing
it here; and to conclude from it, that in proportion as thefe different apprehenfions difcovered
our weaknefs, a firm eftablifhment with the principal powers in our neighbourhood would add to
our ftrength.

In this belief, and in compliance with your
defire, I have reflected much upon the fubject of
forming a confederacy with thefe powers; and
for that purpofe I have examined, as far as my
poor abilities will allow me, all the arguments
that have been urged againft fuch a plan. Before
I attempt to anfwer them, I will acknowledge to
you, that if the queftion was, Whether the Company fhall or fhall not extend their political connexions on the coaft of Coromandel, their trade
and their dominions being as well fecured to
them now, and as free from being difturbed, as
they poffibly can be rendered by any extenfion
of their connexions ?—I would be foremoft in
saying,

354786

saying, that nothing but wild ambition could hefitate upon the fubject.

But as the experience of all countries, and particularly of India, tells us, that where there is no balance eftablifhed there muft necefſarily be contention, until fome one power gains a decided fuperiority over the reft ; and as the Company, it is to be believed, never will aſpire at a domi-nion extenfive enough for that, the queftion now is, Whether they will fuffer any other power to obtain this afcendency? or, Whether they will take advantage of the unexpected and moft fortunate opportunity which is now opened to them, for eftablifhing a balance, and holding the fcale in their own hands? There are but few, I think, who will hefitate in declaring for the former; and the general voice will be to demand, how this can be eftablifhed?

Were I to anfwer fuch a queftion, it fhould be by defiring that public minifters might be fent directly to the Soubah's court, and to that of Hyder-ally, with orders to correfpond together, and with the minifter at the Maratta court, and all feparately with the prefidency of Madras, which being the refidence of the Nabob of the Carnatic, fhould be confidered as the feat of political government on the Peninfula, ftill fubject to

the

the controuling power of the Supreme Council
of Bengal.

But I may be told, that hitherto neither the
poffeffions of the Company, nor of the Nabob,
have been invaded without provocation; and
that as our united ftrength has been encreafing,
while that of the Marattas has been wafting by
their divifions and cabals, it may be hoped that
by leaving things to themfelves, they may work
into a fyftem; or that the difagreements amongft
the other powers, may weaken them fo much as
to throw the afcendancy into our hands.

Thofe, however, who have read the records
of the Company, will not fay this, for they
know, that although the poffeffions of the Nabob, and of the Company, have not been invaded without provocation; that yet they have
been often threatened, and that if the extraordinary abilities of Hyder Ally, joined to the great
refources he had for money, had not made the
Marrattas fufpend hoftilities againft him (I think
it was in 1771) and if the death of Mahadirow,
their Chieftain, had not foon followed this; the
Carnatic, as well as Hyder's country, might by
this time have been in their hands.

Nor will thofe who know any thing of the
character of Hyder Ally, and of the immenfe
ftrides

strides he has made since the death of Mahadirow, say, that our apprehensions should cease,
because the greatness of the Marattas is no more.
Let any one look to the situation of Hyder's
dominions, spreading almost from coast to coast
of the Peninsula, I might have said entirely, for
the Guntoor Circar, with its port, will always be
open to him, whilst Bazalet Jung lives ; and let
any one reflect what a government so compact,
rich in all kinds of productions, and ruled by
such a man as Hyder Ally, or as his son Tippo
Saib, at the head of the best established Black
army that has ever been seen in India, is capable
of doing.

Let him reflect that this government must
necessarily increase in power and strength, as that
of the Marattas declines, from the cessions which
will be made to it, and the seizures it will itself
make from the dominions of that power ; that
the Soubah's weak, and comparatively with Hyder's, defenceless state, may afterwards render
him an easy prey ; and that with these additions
of strength, Hyder may fall upon our northern
Circars, and upon the Carnatic at the same time ;
that with the Circars and the Carnatic, we have
a neck of coast of near eight hundred miles from
North East to South to defend, and a slip of

country

country of near four hundred miles from East to West, and both coast and country skirted by the possessions of Hyder Ally.

Let any one reflect on these circumstances, and then say, whether our apprehensions should cease, because the Maratta greatness is no more. He will, I think, rather say, that a much greater power is rising up, and that all may be endangered, if timely measures are not taken to prevent it.

I think too he will confess that no other measure can be effectual, but that of establishing a balance of power, by dividing and yet upholding the Marattas; by strengthening the Soubah, in obtaining for him the districts which they have promised to cede to him; by getting a grant as soon as possible from him of the Guntoor Circar; by establishing a respectable black cavalry, under the command of the Company's officers; by becoming principals through the medium of our own agents at the several courts, still acting in concert with the Nabob; and by lending a military assistance to the Soubah, for the ESTABLISHMENT OF ORDER in his own government; the expence to be deducted from the annual tribute for the Circars, which, upon the cession of that of Guntoor, will become seven

F   lacks

lacks of rupees, and the releafe from which would certainly be the reward of the fervices the Soubah would receive, in point of finance and authority, from the affiftance of our troops.

By thefe means, and by continuing a detachment with the Marattas, we fhould not only infure thofe two powers in our intereft, but from the influence that would give us, obtain a confideration with Hyder, which might make him feek for an intimate connection with us, with as much warmth as he did in 1771, when he was fo preffed by the Marattas, as I have before obferved.

It has been faid that the fort of Trichinopoly is a check upon Hyder on one fide, and that the Bombay government bridles him on the other; and I know this opinion has prevailed, and with reafon, fo far as thofe terms mean the preventing him from extending his conquefts either in the neighbourhood of the fort of Trichinopoly, or of that of Bombay.

But we have no reafon as yet to fear any attempts to take our forts from us; what we have to apprehend is, that our countries may be laid wafte from year to year, and neither Bombay nor Trichinopoly (if Trichinopoly, inftead of a ruin, was as ftrong as Bombay) could prevent

vent Hyder or the Marattas from doing this,
whenever either fhould be tempted to difregard us.

For what protection can a garrifon give to a
country that is open almoft on every fide, when
large armies of cavalry break in to lay it wafte?
All our troops can do in fuch cafes, is to extend
their protection for a few miles around their
forts, and to fhelter the poor inhabitants who
may fly from their defolated villages to feek
fecurity for the little they may bring away with
them.

But if we are in clofe alliance with Hyder
Ally, the Marattas cannot difturb us in the Carnatic, becaufe to do it they muft pafs through
his country; and if we are in alliance with
them, we can have nothing to fear from him on
the Malabar fide, where they are all powerful;
and the Soubah lying between both, muft, as a
friend, be a kind of barrier againft each of them,
and ftrengthened as we fhould ftrengthen him,
would be a great check upon them both.

But it may be urged, that the Company's
troops fhould be kept as much together as pof-
fible, and that the ftationing any part at Hydra-
bad, or any where in the Soubah's dominions,
would be removing them too far from the coaft,
and that in cafe of an alarm from the French

very bad confequences might attend this. And certainly, if the queftion was fimply, Whether the Company's troops would be in better order and difcipline, and better prepared to refift an invafion from the French, when kept together near Madras, than when divided, the anfwer would be felf-evident.

. But as this can never be the queftion, while we have fuch a powerful neighbour as Hyder encircling us on all fides; as to guard againft him, troops muft always be kept in Tanjore, Trichinopoly, and Tennevelly, the latter of which is four hundred miles from Madras; as the Circars, befides the forts upon the fea coaft, which extend fix hundred miles from Madras, ought to have a back fupport, and as the centre of the Soubah's dominions is but about three hundred miles from Mafulipatam on one fide, and not five hundred miles from Bombay on the other; I confefs I do not fee any more danger to be apprehended from ftationing a detachment with the Soubah, we having the funds in our own hands for paying it, than there is in ftationing one in Tanjore.

At leaft the great advantages of eftablifhing and keeping the balance of power in our own hands; the immediate poffeffion of the Guntoor Circar; and from it of a revenue of £100,000 more, ap-

pear

pear to me fo greatly to counter-balance every objection that can be urged againft the meafure, that I am perfuaded, if ever it is thoroughly confidered, they muft prevail for its eftablifh-ment.

It may be faid, all this may be very juft, but that yet, as the plan is a very extenfive one, the fentiments of the Supreme Council, and of the Prefidencies of Madras and Bombay, fhould be received upon it, before it is attempted to put it in execution; and that as we are now in per-feét peace, encreafing in riches and in ftrength, no bad confequences can attend the waiting for fuch farther explanations as the public advices from the feveral prefidencies may give.

I know arguments of this kind are often ufed, and fometimes even by thofe who wifh well to the public, and have minds capable of difcerning its true intereft, but who want refo-lution to bring forward their fentiments when the novelty and boldnefs of them make it pro-bable that they may be oppofed.

To fuch men one might fay, revolutions in India are often but the work of a day; that the Marattas, who but five years ago made all the other powers on the peninfula tremble, are now in need of being fupported; that Hyder Ally, who not longer ago was almoft reduced to naked-nefs,

nefs, is now a moft formidable power; that the
Company, having undertaken the mediation between the Marattas, are bound, as much in intereft as honour, to prevent the interference of any
other power for that purpofe; that Hyder is
ready, on one fide, to feize upon thofe diftricts
of their country which adjoin to his own; whilft
the Soubah, on the other, fide, is prepared to
take poffeffion of thofe which they have ceded;
or rather engaged to reftore to him; that the Company are under feparate defenfive engagements
with the Soubah and with Hyder; and that now
being engaged in the fame manner to the Marattas, they are actually involved in all the extent
of the fyftem.

It is worth ftopping a little here to fee how,
without any plan laid down, without any concert
between the prefidencies of Madras and Bombay,
without any uniform principle of conduct even
in the government of Madras, the Company have
been imperceptibly embarked, and that for the
moft part of neceffity too, in the political fyftem
of the peninfula. This fact is the argument
which fhould be given to thofe who, though convinced themfelves, want ftrength of mind enough
to undertake the conviction of others.

To fmooth the way for them a little, we may
add, that as local knowledge, and a perfonal ac-
quaintance

quaintance with the intrigues and intriguing men
about courts, muſt neceſſarily give great advantages to a miniſter; and that, on the contrary,
as the want of ſuch information muſt ſubjeƈt him
to difficulties, and poſſibly lead him into errors;
the Company cannot begin too ſoon to procure
theſe advantages to themſelves; and that therefore the appointment of miniſters to the ſeveral
courts ſhould be immediately made upon the
general grounds of policy, the great points to be
left for farther refleƈtion; if, after ſeeing our-
ſelves abſolutely embarked, and knowing the
great advantages the preſent opportunity affords
us, it ſhould ſtill remain a doubt, whether we
ſhould now take meaſures for ſecuring the balance of power, and for holding the ſcale in our
own hands.

* * * * * * * * *

F I N I S.

www.ingramcontent.com/pod-product-compliance
Lightning Source LLC
Chambersburg PA
CBHW032119080426
42733CB00008B/993